T0336303

uninvited

un invited

talking

back

to

Plato

Carrie Jenkins *and* Carla Nappi

McGill-Queen's University Press

Montreal & Kingston · London · Chicago

ISBN 978-0-2280-0131-7 (cloth)
ISBN 978-0-2280-0269-7 (ePDF)
ISBN 978-0-2280-0270-3 (ePUB)

Legal deposit second quarter 2020
Bibliothèque nationale du Québec

Printed in Canada on acid-free paper that is 100% ancient forest free
(100% post-consumer recycled), processed chlorine free

We acknowledge the support of the Canada Council for the Arts.

Nous remercions le Conseil des arts du Canada de son soutien.

Library and Archives Canada Cataloguing in Publication

Title: Uninvited : talking back to Plato / Carrie Jenkins and Carla
    Nappi.
Other titles: Uninvited (Montréal, Québec) | Talking back to Plato
Names: Container of (work): Jenkins, Carrie. Poems. Selections. |
    Container of (work): Nappi, Carla Suzan, 1977– Poems. Selections.
Identifiers: Canadiana (print) 2020017729X | Canadiana
    (ebook) 2020017732X | ISBN 9780228001317 (cloth) | ISBN
    9780228002697 (ePDF) | ISBN 9780228002703 (ePUB)
Subjects: LCSH: American poetry—21st century.
Classification: LCC PS617 .U55 2020 | DDC 811/.608—dc23

Set in 11/14 Mrs Eaves
Book design & typesetting by Garet Markvoort, zijn digital

Contents

Prefatory Note

Our practice as scholars is open to the creation of artistic works as a way of thinking with ideas, texts, and situations. We find this approach generative, often opening possibilities not accessible by other means.

These poems are a product of this practice. They were composed in conversation with, and in reaction to, Plato's *Symposium*, working with the 1989 translation by Alexander Nehamas and Paul Woodruff. *Symposium* is essentially a series of speeches about love, delivered by a series of men. In making space for other sorts of voices, our poems can be understood as extending, responding to, or metamorphosing Plato's text.

Throughout this text, you will find what are called Stephanus numbers (178A, etc.). These refer to sections of *Symposium*. If you prefer to experience our text in conversation with that of Plato, these numbers can guide you to moments in the *Symposium* text that inspired us. If you prefer not to read our pieces that way, feel free to consider the numbers simply as precipitates of the processes that generated our poems.

However you choose to experience this text – on a beach or a bus, spoken aloud or silently, alongside Plato's *Symposium* or on its own – thank you for spending time with it.

Acknowledgments

This book would not have been possible without the generosity and care of the community that grew with and around it. We thank our loved ones, our Arts One students, our amazing roomful of manuscript workshoppers, and our editor Khadija Coxon for the sustained and nourishing attention that helped to bring the book into being.

uninvited

Many-voiced

> *The path on which the initiate is drawn is described in line 2*
> *of Parmenides' poem with the surprising adjective πολύφημον —*
> *"many-saying" or "many-voiced."*
> Jan Zwicky, "Why Is Diotima a Woman?"

in fact, your question does not find me unprepared
              me unprepared   in fact, your question does
                        not find me
          the most worthless man on earth
but this is how nehamas and woodruff told it to us through many
    voices

once upon a very beginning
        the very beginning

                              of course

        of course
              of course
of course
              translators like us
              [not like us]
              [not translators] anyway

the speeches went something like this
                              who has a better right than
                        you to report
                        his
                        conversation
          let her play for herself, or, if she prefers, for the women
            in the house

what if
> she prefers
> the women in the house
>> were you there yourself?
> it really was a long time ago
>> aristodemus couldn't
>> remember
> and I myself don't remember
i really don't like crowds
> and i really don't like doctors
funny thing is just the other day

i woke up crying
blood: apparently it's a thing
in hell dimensions i said but my doctor said
haha no, just like a nosebleed
out of your eyes and i said *are you kidding me*
and she said i shouldn't worry and i said
everybody says that

> the truth is
what's wrong with me
> who knows, if i touch you, i may catch a bit of the wisdom
>> who knows if
>> i touch you
it's not transmitted that way

> i'm a maniac, and i'm raving
> but i'd better tell you the whole story
>> not mine the tale
> yours is bright and radiant and has a splendid
> future

with these words, they set out

178A.

I was there when the gods died. I came to unmake my son.

178B.

He came third. It was Chaos, and the Earth, and then Love.
Chaos was first and was everything and was alone. Earth had a
broad chest, and people sat on him, and they were safe there.
Love was designed by a goddess.

And we know this because of the agreement of the men. Because
knowledge is what happens when men agree. And this is how
history is made.

And so there was everything, and then there was safety, and
finally there was design. And we know nothing of everything
except that it was first. And what we know of safety is that it was
useful. And once there was everything, and once it was useful,
then there was intention, and with intention came the first
woman of the story, and she was a designer. And so from the
beginning, the history of woman is the history of manipulation.

*He was love, and I came to him and sat with him and
took him apart into refuge and disarray. (Chaos sang a
dirge that drove me mad, for a bit, and Earth held me
while I shook.) And then he was gone. And then safety
was gone, and then there was only everything and I was
alone with everything.*

178C.

All sides agree, then.

I had nothing.

178D.

With the woman came love, and with love came shame, and with
shame came pain.

And that pain was the pain of being seen.

And that pain was the pain of not being seen.

And so the eyes carved public from private with the hot knife of a
glance and the "me" was made in blood and bubbling fat.

And shame and shame and shame and shame, lovers made of
shame, families made of shame, cities made of shame, and shame
and shame and shame and shame and shame and shame.

> *I sat in his death and raised hands to eyes and looked for*
> *him in the darkness but now there was no I to look or to*
> *be seen and so I became everything. Flesh into soil breath*
> *into wind, heart beating a tectonic pulse, translucent*
> *language rippling the sand as it arced and dipped.*

178E.

And shame and shame and shame and shame.

We are misbehaving prey, we are hunters.

We are soldiers at war, we are comrades in arms.

We are a city of lovers made lovers made beloved by shame and
shame and shame and shame and shame and shame and shame
and shame.

> *The language puts its fingers to your lips — its fingers*
> *do not belong to it, she has become everything now*
> *and everything cannot have, everything cannot*
> *own, everything cannot possess or covet, love is dead*
> *there are no gods now, no selves, no she, so let us*
> *say there simply are fingers and they are at your lips*
> *which are not yours, not anymore — and they urge,*
> *Shhhhhhhhhhhhhhhhhhhhhhhh, listen and be quiet and*
> *disappear for a little while feel it it's nice isn't it.*

179A.
Even a few of us, in battle side by side, would conquer all the world, I'd say.

> *Yes they are still lips if they are not your lips. Yes they are fingers. (Flex them.) They are not your fingers. Your lovers. Your cities. Your territory to conquer. Your prey your gods your earth your everything your goddess your mother your woman. They are not yours.*

179B.
No one will die for you but a lover.

> *No one will die for you.*

179C.
They will estrange you from your family. (Let them.) They will flay your parents to bones and names. (Let them.) They will take your death from you. (Let them.)
The gods will be delighted.

> *You must do that for yourself.*

179D.
Once upon a time, Orpheus went to hell to claim a woman he was a musician he was soft he arrived alive.
(He would not die for her. He would not die for you.)
And hell sneered and ruddied and kept the woman and taunted the man and showed him her picture and sent him back to be ripped apart by maenads the end.

> *Perhaps the women will help.*

179E.

Once upon a time there was Achilles. His mother told him he would die if he killed the man who killed his lover but he did it anyway and died happily ever after the end.

> *The women will not help. Here they are — mothers killing sons, maenads killing musicians — afterthoughts and plot devices, fortunetellers and photographs. They are not your mothers, your photos, your wives, your seers, your murderers. No one bothers asking what they want. Follow the trail of women, here. You follow death. It only ever ends one way.*

180A.

He was just a boy.
The gods were delighted.

180B.

> *I was there when the gods died. I came to unmake my son.*

180C.

> *And then I did more. I unmade the world and myself and I became everything and no one and I showed you that you are everything and no one and then we were more and more and more and more.*
> *But no one could remember those very well.*
> *So they skipped them and moved on to other things.*

180C—D.

Lesson 1: On the kind of love that ought to be praised

Hush, now. My turn.   *I'm not sure, this —*

You're doing it wrong.

Watch me.

Shut up.   *But, it —*

Watch me.

Stop crying.

Give me your hand.

Do you see these two fingers? Yes?   *No, I —*

Can you feel them? That tightness as I push them apart?

And what if I keep pushing?

And what about now?

And now?

(Stop crying. Just stop it.)

And … there.

Do you feel that?   *No.*

Shush. Now close your eyes.   *No.*

Don't look at your hand. Just feel.   *I don't think —*

Now.   *No.*

That's not pleasant, is it?   *No.*

No, it's not, is it.   *I said no.*

That's painful.

Keep your eyes closed.

Now, do you feel that?   …

Isn't that beautiful?   …

180E.

Lesson 2: On the importance of keeping the gods apart

Here is a rock.

Open your eyes. Look at it.

It's just a rock. (That's all it is.)

Now watch me touch it.

Do you see how the rock changes?

Can you see how I change the rock?

Do you see how the rock becomes beautiful?

Watch now, while I do this to it.

…

Do you see how it becomes repulsive?

(The world is like this rock. It's perfect without us. Just by existing, we make it beautiful and disgusting.)

(Just by existing, you make the world imperfect. Isn't that something?)

Now touch the rock.

…

Why won't you touch the rock?

…

…

Maybe we should have sent the flute girl away.

181A.

Lesson 3: On having a choice

There's nothing wrong with what we're doing.

…

I love you.

181B.

Lesson 4: On the love felt by the vulgar

It's you that brings this out in me.

181C.

Lesson 5: On finding pleasure in what is by nature stronger and more intelligent

Exercise: Find a quiet spot to stand. Make yourself comfortable and be still. Close your eyes. Stay that way until you can hear the sound of your body aging. Open your eyes. Now do your best to try to forget that sound.

181D.

Lesson 6: On signs that they have begun to form minds of their own
Vocabulary:

To be
To fall
To prefer
To show
To begin
To form
To convince
To prepare
To share
To love
To spend
To aim
To deceive
To take advantage
To expose
To move on to someone else

181E.

Lesson 7: On wasting time and effort on an uncertain pursuit
Once there was a girl.
She played the flute.
She came to a room where there were men and couches to learn
about love.
(That's not why they invited her.)
(She didn't play the flute very well.)
She sat and she listened. She sat as still as stone and made her
skin into pumice and her flesh a stone sponge and she closed
stony lids over stony eyes and opened pores for the words to
seep through and she listened and listened and the words came
through her skin and into her mouth and she felt them in
her belly and then she was full of the words of the men on the
couches until her flesh began to flake and flow into consonants

and vowels and then she was words and when the men spoke they were speaking her and she was their language and she sounded like music and the men on the couches looked at one another and they were afraid.

182A.
Lesson 8: On doing things properly and in accordance with our customs
Exercise: Notice the others in the room. Look to your right. Now look behind you. Touch your own hot hand. Understand that you have all become volcanoes. She is the fevered language spewing tectonic from you.

182B.
Lesson 9: On saving oneself the trouble of having to offer reasons
I burn as I flow through you, don't I.

Does it hurt?

Poor baby.

Show me where it hurts.

…

Yes I am laughing at you. I am your laughter. I am laughing myself through you.

Would you prefer that I kept speaking instead?

Does that make it hurt less?

But I am just a poor speaker, born in an inarticulate place.

…

No one there would ever consider this shameful.

182C.
Lesson 10: On being no good for rulers
Yes, you probably should have sent me away.

182D—E.

Lesson 11: On encouraging a lover in every possible way

The more open we can be about these things, the better.

You see, there's two of us.

Like I explained before.

(Was it me who explained that?)

And one of us is shameful. And secretive.

And one of us knows how to be open about these things.

(You know how to be open about these things, don't you. I've always admired that about you people.)

…

There's this rock, you see.

Pick up the rock.

I'll wait.

…

Now hold the rock in your hand.

What do you feel when you feel the rock?

Now put it against your ear.

What do you hear when you hear the rock?

Does it speak to you?

Does it sound like me?

When you hear me, do you feel we are two, do you feel we are separate? Do you feel estranged from your language?

And are you ashamed, yet?

Put the rock in your mouth.

183A.

Lesson 12: On being willing to do what lovers do for the ones they love

But rocks melt in the mouths of volcanoes.

And so the rock melts.

And she repeats it, inside the language of the others, and so all of the rocks in all of the mouths melt until there are no more rocks and all the mouths are gone and then she must speak instead through their hands.

183B.

Lesson 13: On what a charming man he is
Vocabulary:

    Grasp

    Beg

    Pray

    Offer

    Wring

    Unclasp

    Slap

    Stroke

183C.

Lesson 14: On the lover's desire and the willingness to satisfy it
Once there was a room of hot mouthless men on couches who
could only speak in a handlanguage that was actually a flute girl.
(Can you imagine what it must be like to be someone else's
language, to only be that.)
(Every time they spoke, they would speak you into being.)
(When they were silent, you would exist only as past and
potential.)
(In their silence you would be only memory and desire.)
(Can you imagine only existing as someone's memory or desire.)
(Only one of you could be inside any now: any given
moment could not sustain the two of you existing, voiced,
simultaneously.)
...
(This was not a new thing, actually, for the flute girl.)

183D.

Lesson 15: On knowing who counts as vile in this context
And so speaking with their hands she raised fingers to faces and
scratched and tore mouths into them once again.

But all that came out was steam and hiss and vomiting liquid stone.

...

(This was not a new thing, truth be told, for the flute girl.)

183E.

Lesson 16: On loving the mutable and unstable

And so the flute girl became steam, and she became hiss, and she became the liquid stone spewing from the holes that were the mouths of the volcanoes on the couches.

184A.

Lesson 17: On seeing the point of our customs

Exercise: Compose an essay on one of the following themes, as it relates to volcanoes and their language —

> *On separating the wheat from the chaff*
> *On doing everything we can to make it as easy as possible*
> *On a kind of test to determine to which sort each belongs*
> *On yielding too quickly*
> *On the passage of time in itself*
> *On being seduced*

184B—C.

Lesson 18: On deciding to put oneself at another's disposal

One man did not become a volcano. Instead, he became the mouth of a river.

The girl made of language scooped sand from his body and dropped it into the mouths of the other men, and made glass beads that way, and she would have strung them all into a necklace, if she had a body to drape it on, but she did not and so instead she made the beads part of her.

And the next time the volcanoes spoke, they erupted in a language of glass beads.

184D.

Lesson 19: On each obeying the principle appropriate to him

And thus their language was in countable units that could be owned and exchanged.

And thus the flute girl became their property once again.

184E.

Lesson 20: On being taught and improved by a lover

And so they divided her up amongst themselves.

Each took a bit of her, and they put her back in their mouths and melted the glass of her back into a liquid that cooled their flames and hushed their hissing and glazed their stony flows with a smooth blue.

And slowly they got their language back.

There, now that's better, one said as he recognized his reflection mirrored in the glazing of his friend across the room.

Here is a rock, he said, and cradled it with his hand, and picked it up, and threw it.

185A.

Lesson 21: On taking a lover in the mistaken belief that this lover is a good man

Exercise: *Do your best to put the pieces of yourself back together again.*

            ...

        We'll wait.

185B.

Lesson 22: On it being noble to have been deceived

I really feel like we've learned something today.

185C.

Lesson 23: On my contribution to the subject of love

Examination

    Question 1:

    Once there was a girl.

    She played the flute.

    She came to a room where

    there were men and couches to learn about love.

    What would you teach the girl, about love?

185D.

Lesson 24: On holding your breath for as long as you possibly can

Examination

    Question 2:

    And would she survive the lesson?

185E.

Lesson 25: On curing even the most persistent case

Examination

    Question 3:

    And would you?

I'm a Doctor

185E—186A.
If I have learned a single lesson from my own field
    it's that infinite regress is all the rest
we get. Arithmetic or Love: it doesn't matter which path you
   prefer
and here endeth the lesson.
    it's that we make maps to know our heavenly
bodies: Love too will be labelled
on a doctor's diagram. A medical student
once told me corpses
can really party. *That* I said
sure endeth the lesson.
    it's that History will give us all
the wrong names. This lesson like all my best bad days
endeth in aporia.
    it's that we want Geography
to say exactly where Love lives. Our Natural Sciences
to be our Moral Sciences. Well, all I can do
is draw. Blood or cards? Let me treat you.
First (or before that) the Fool, whose lesson
is never allowed to begin.

186B.
The second step might as well be infinite. And *that's*
how a number can fool you. Trust nothing.
Certainly
not your senses. You see even

in the world of plants health is no empirical
matter. My mind the rotten castle is breaking
its promises. *Healthy* is a safe old house
barfing its wormy little wooden insides
out through the basement windows,
shedding that brown earthy cellar-
smell all over the street, gashes exposed in a once-living-
room wall, oozing rust from a pipe, a twisted
colon, perhaps iron. Once an important conduit,
now infected, scabbed, leaking bubbly orange pus. Sick
if you say so. I say showing signs.
Skull-like, come November I may switch to my winter skin
and refit this highly marketable property. *Disease*. Like us,
part-language. It occurs everywhere in the universe. What else
to call this spinning crystal of dead truths? All light
and values. Inside, tiny hands claw at something
scarlet and empty. Could be a complicated
birth. Don't rush.

186C.

O ye men, how can it be but women should be strong,
seeing they do thus?
Zorobabel, 1 Esdras Chapter 4

It is shameful to consort with the debauched.
In our cups we three turn
tail: swirl sweet and sick, candy-
orange, excess red, a grey-haired
shush. *Suck on it.* We are grown
women, so rich the blood
on our expensive gowns defines a grin, bone-teeth
through stretchy coverings. Oh boys
who died and made you! Such nights,
what it is to be an expert in medicine.

186D.

October crows snatch at a filthy
blanket of leafstuff, costume for some Dickens orphan
with a snot-cobweb for a face. The street's silver
skin shivers through in bare
patches. Wait, no:
some of it is a rat. We try to look at the stars
through its eyes – well it's not using them –
but they've been dead too long.
The stars I mean. We squabble over eyeballs
and star-dust while semantic overload burns
the goth birds out. Our vocal fry
turns chronic. *For Love's sake*, we sigh in leaving,
let things end. And that's the hallmark
of the accomplished physician.

186E.

Our ancestor Asclepius first
[fuck founding fathers] established medicine
as a profession when he learned how to produce concord
and love between such opposites.
Now how to get its sick *beak*
out of my business. Cloaking befits its grim
visits to this black bed, too tiny
for my plague. Three-fifths of me
are dead already – I don't mourn them, I want
to talk terms. How much meat
exactly do I cut off to get rid of you. Speak up,
I said specifics. Will you accept
my art my skull my ego my bank details
my home that was. How long
does all that buy me. What dies
before I do – my sense of self my voice
my internet connection. I saw a specialist
who said the wait list is out
of this world. I said the time between attacks

is getting shorter. She said if that's true
you must make your own peace.

187A–B.

On being guided everywhere by the god of Love
A voice at variance with itself
is in agreement with itself "like the attunement of a bow or
lyre." Lyre. LYRE.
Say it three times to a broken mirror. Sappho appears! [speak to
    me]
Discordant elements, as long as they are still
in discord, cannot come to an agreement
[yes and]
people who make money peddling paradoxes
don't want them resolved [just someone
to remember us]
right [even in another time]
right. The case of music and poetry, too, is exactly the same:
we did it all for someone
else's coins and memories
[but you have forgotten me] well,
I'm a doctor not a necromancer.
Diagnosis: *pants on fire*.

187C.

On the effects of Love on rhythm and harmony
Do this: when you're out on a busy
street start stepping sideways. Channel
your inner crab. Do it today. What happens
when you put your crabby claw
through norms nobody cares
to see. Feel your chest first – does it hurt,
tickle – but don't forget your eyes,
how things far away stay still and close ones
move. Listen:

crystal spheres, moral universes
were shattered by that. Can you imagine?
Now sing, since you're all out of tune.
Do it today.

187D.

complications arise
This is getting serious. We're out
of phase with the sun. The sky. Standing dead
still. *It's not you* I whisper out the window
it's us but either way
we can hardly discuss the musicality of education
when time itself has unfriended the room.
We should have given it better gifts. Now these meetings
are where scholarly dreams go to die.
Ours are replacing the perpetually motionless xerox machine
and getting the mould scraped off our office walls.
Each time the identical argument. Our symposiasts
are good people, or those whom such love
might improve. I find the gaps
between reality and what we imagine
blue and fuzzy, like little oceans.
They require the treatment of a good practitioner.
But tune in to the background. Somewhere on campus,
a student is practising his sad trombone.

187E.

Ourania (The Hermit)
I am old, that's the main thing.
Don't talk about hell to someone
halfway down. These days I see
double: faith
in the beauty of crumbling temples,
the blank vacuum of sunk investments. Drilling
migraines pay for my vision. Would it kill us marble

statues if we all danced, did something
with a little spirit? Even if it's for one night,
a costume. What are clothes
anyway? What's skin? My lamp flickers:
every chance has always been
a one-time offer. *Act now!*
Extreme caution is indicated.

188A.

the seasons of the year exhibit their influence
My winter skin is paler, a lily for the dead
light. Was it this wrinkled last spring
when I put it away? No problem, I needed
to get the iron out. I work nights
while odd clocks spin the darkness
into warm clothes. Fortune finds me:
more time. Forwards? Call it that. Round and
round
       and
            round
she goes. The arrow in this body aims
to live. One more year?
Look up (call it that): continuum-many
more. Parsimony is a desert's
virtue and you my dear are still green.
Still full of it. Poison and possibility.
What is the matter
with this medicine.

188B.

(Page of Cups)
He spreads the plague –
must have caught it in school.
I mean from TV. Video games. Religion
and the lack of it. The presence

and absence of a strong father figure. Not from *us*.
This immodest and disordered boy couldn't have drunk
toxins *here*. Despite resembling Chaos
and contrary to many myths
He has not always existed.
Actually He is not shapeless
at all and not even very old. Only now
the stars and the seasons are afraid of Him.

188C.
(Knight of Swords)
Grown to manhood He smells of clementine
and spiced tobacco. Flame
and spur. His flannel
shirts and beard are clean, he even wears
product
and the women won't help.
With their ways and ways
and ways of making Him miserable. The main one
is doing nothing. This is not
what was written, not how His future
was told to Him for hundreds of years
when He was little. *Women.* In His clementine mind
He prepares to banish them all to an island
of lesbians. But He forgets
to do it, distracted by eternally looping
fantasies in which they're all looking at the camera,
never each other.

188D—E.
Absence makes the heart
In the future, I'm a doctor.
Today, you have drawn the Queen Of Swords
who was made royal with sorrow.
When her turquoise robe sprouted clouds,

her head and hands were left floating:
weapon and bracelet, crown
and tears. But everything inside the cloak
rejoined the sky, became the space
that once defined her outlines.
Perhaps I, too, have omitted a great deal
in this discourse on Love.

188E—189C.
Use your head!
The King's prayer to the Queen:
Let me "unsay what I have
said." If I could remake the snow, blank
for better footprints ...
She answers: *Don't put up your guard*
against me. Penitence
comes with the territory — these marks
are the traces of my Muse. If it's suddenly winter,
at least your hiccups seem cured.

Before Aristophanes

Zero.
Have you ever gone into space?
Up there, on a good day and from the right angle, you can almost see what we used to look like.

One.
Down here there are no good days and no right angles.
To punish us, we were split and this is the history of what we call selves.
The break was messy.
Bleeding.
Solitary confinement, as we all pretend we don't know, is a form of torture.
Like sensory deprivation, only not for a body's senses.
Cruel.
And unusual, once.
It's amazing what you can make usual if you try.
If we all really try.
In a desperate effort to return to being whole we have started seeing things.
Nations.
Universities.
Football teams.
Women.
Our failed "we"s created intensely painful "they"s and were created by them and this is the history of hate.
I think I said hate I meant love.
I think I said love I meant war.
I think I said we.

We no longer understand what one means because knowing that would kill us.

But when we are nine-tenths asleep a hundredth of us can half remember what it is not.

That it is neither each nor all.

That it does not have an arithmetic, which would surprise many of us though maybe not the monks who call themselves our mathematicians.

Two.

Because we are afraid of understanding one we animate ourselves with the idea of two.

Animation is making a picture breathe.

We make moving pictures of two and we try to breathe in these pictures like using a paper bag to calm a panic attack and this is the history of art.

It never fixed anything, any more than old Sawbones over here ever healed anyone.

Were you hoping it would?

Three.

A few days after the division we started seeing women and then men and then there was nothing left in our imaginations.

Three, we began to say, is a crowd of third wheels.

Too big to stay in any hotel room and not big enough to believe in.

As if acknowledging three might damage two.

Make two feel small.

Three point one four one five nine.

The division did not proceed along rational lines.

Nobody is sure what we're being punished for, but it must have been something terrible and wonderful and we have spent a few centuries fighting about what exactly it could have been and whom exactly we could have offended and this is the history of religions.

Above all we feel there should be some numerical clue.

A key to understanding all cycles.

Life and death, day and night, digestion, abuse, agriculture, blood, laundry, and the moon.

A key that would unlock our spinning crystal prison.

There isn't.

Four.

We made should as a cushion for isn't and this is the history of value.

We put it in the stars along with the future.

But should turned out to be quite edgy too.

Should hurt just as much when it burrowed in through our ribcages and stuck like a black mass to our lungs until we couldn't breathe in the old pictures any more.

Counting breaths is another strategy for dealing with a panic attack if you do not have a paper bag handy.

Or you can do it to measure how long a body has been alive.

Animated.

Five.

Keep breathing.

Six.

There's nothing special about six so let's take a look at the letters instead.

S. I. X.

Are they beautiful?

How about VI?

We used to mistake letters for numbers but we have been getting better at counting.

Counting has been necessary since the division though honestly we have not mastered the skill.

Somewhere in a remote monastery an order of cloistered mathematicians has been counting under its breath continuously since the division.

Day shift, night shift.

When one monk dies another monk is born.

Every day they can count twice as fast as the day before.

But as they get faster and faster they count in smaller and smaller subdivisions, so it doesn't really help.

We do not know what would happen to us if the monks stopped counting and this is the history of time.

Seven.

At some point in the past, present, or future, the division will be called a natural event and an explosion.

It will be argued that we did it to ourselves and that nobody did it and this will be the history of science.

And we will make weeks in order to have weekends.

It is something to look forward.

Eight.

If you see a body dying you should breathe into it like a paper bag to calm the panic attack you are having.

Count one Mississippi two Mississippi.

This is also a good way of achieving immortality because those two seconds will go on forever.

Once you are immortal, come back and tell us what happened after the monks stopped counting.

Never tell us what one means.

Nine.

I have forgotten what happened.

Long ago we were united, as I said.

One theory is we didn't split cleanly and that is why we leak.

Ten.

Now don't get ideas.

Love does the best that can be done for the time being.

Don't make a comedy of it.

A Crown for Aphrodite

One.

> *If, on the contrary, two stars should really be situated very near each other, and at the same time so far insulated as not to be materially affected by the attractions of neighbouring stars, they will then compose a separate system, and remain united by the bond of their own mutual gravitation towards each other.*
>
> William Herschel

This is the count of every thing. One, two.
The self, the other. Day, night. Here and there.
Two stars, one system, struck with cosmic glue.
Who's in, who's out all turning on this prayer:
Let there be prizes. Order in the strange.
Love settled like success on things that smelled
Of roses, not of grease, of wheels, of change.
Beholder's gazing subdued the beheld:
Soft skin, pink cheek, hair delicately curled.
Good luck with no umbrella in the rain.
Like beauty, love and justice, and this world,
A self takes time and money to maintain.
    Who gets to play beholder? To be free.
    To win. To be the winner. Hey, it's me!

Two.

To win. To be the winner. Hey, it's me!
The crown's too big. I wear it round my face.
It feels like hiding. I'm not here to see.
I stay still – very still – to keep my place.
It's awful when the only way is down,
There's only fear left, everything's a threat
And nobody's a peer. Love and renown
Cannot be friends. There is no love, just debt.
I want to wear what other women wear:
A gown of purple grapes, a tiny flower.
I want to dance and climb and cut my hair.
I'm tired of eating gold and shitting power.
    We are not comfy where we most belong.
    Toss me that apple and I'll sing a song.

Three.

Toss me that apple and I'll sing a song.
It's mouldy in the middle, full of worms.
I want those worms in me. It makes me strong,
Surrounding death. I'm made of germs
And cancers, skull and gut. The stringy veins
That tie this self together wring its neck.
Give me self-love enough to cut my brains
In two, make life-rafts from the heart-shaped wreck.
Survival isn't victory. It's not.
It's what you love the most on this black earth,
And me, I love to win. I've watched the rot
That is my body ever since my birth
 Grow mighty, know desire, sound the wine sea:
 "To be the chosen one or not to be."

Four.

"To be the chosen one or not to be."
The rage of white men's always a good start.
I'm not your goddess though. My songs aren't free.
"The Heart Attacks: when white men fall apart."
"The End of White Men: Caesar aut nihil."
"White Men Get Thinky: all white in the head."
"All Must Have Prizes: each Jack's earned his Jill."
(That one is filthy. They're white hot in bed.)
I knew so many songs! I'd just begun
When most of them got lost. I'll whisper this:
You asked me how to be the chosen one.
It always was a choice and it still is.
    I've called this epic bullshit all along.
    Y'all who sang before me did it wrong.

Five.

For J–J Rousseau

Y'all who sang before me did it wrong.
Don't we all wish we could go back in time
To ye sweete olde dayes where we'd all belong?
I know: you felt before you thought. No crime,
But god, man, try to think. At least admit
It's not one or the other: mind and heart
Aren't oil and water. If you can't commit
To rhyme with reason, maybe this mad art
Is not for you. I've read the books
Of other men who lie in fancy graves.
Deep time has ruined more than just their looks.
Their tears its marble surface. Tiny waves:
    "But I feel feelings more than all the rest!"
    What's happy if you're not the happiest?

Six.

Can you imagine language, once clear-cut and exact, softening and guttering,
losing shape and import, becoming mere lumps of sound again?
H.G. Wells

The simple tale had become shapeless; he wanted to shake off the thought of it ...
Kafka

What's happy if you're not the happiest?
You're basic, that's what. Nothing in a shirt.
You blend in. You score average on the test.
You're cast as *chorus member*. Does that hurt?
Your voice: an average Joe. No accents please.
Your voice: a neutral witness, bias-free.
Your voice: a lawyer. Endless legalese.
Your voice: a doctor. (Trust him, he's a he.)
With all these voices, still you speak in lumps
Of sound. Your face gets soft, becomes a blob,
A blank mask, whitish clay in empty bumps
With staring holes for eyes and gaping gob.
 What *are* you wearing? Looks one-size-fits-all.
 A skin, a fig-leaf. Fashion for the Fall.

Seven.

A skin, a fig-leaf. Fashion for the Fall.
If menswear does indeed proclaim the men
Inside it then you're fucked. All men. Yes all.
You'll never be respectable again.
You leave without a character. No parts,
And barely whole. This black earth's going to sting
When you get stuck there. When it fills your hearts,
And mouths and eyes and cocks and everything,
Each man *the man alone*. And one by one
You'll reinvent the systems you call "fair,"
Blame everyone but you for what's been done
And die and rot and nobody will care.
    I've seen you naked and I'm not impressed.
    Let's ask Coco Chanel who wore it best.

Eight.

Let's ask Coco Chanel who wore it best.
"A war's the time for fashion. Seize your chance:
Dress women all in black. That's if they're dressed
At all." And she should know. The circumstance
Dictates the yarn, a pattern's cut in time,
And womenswear like tree-rings prints its past
In languages of flowers and mad rhyme.
Designerless. The skin should give way last:
We'll layer an inch thick over Yorick's grin
To get the natural look. Our face the ground
For battle after battle. Please, jump in.
Parisian judgment makes the world go round.
    We must respond, whoever makes the call:
    Youth's beauty, beauty youth – and that is all.

Nine.

Youth's beauty, beauty youth – and that is all.
A child collecting pebbles on the shore:
A kidney. Half a heart. A gristle ball.
A grey-blue steak of driftwood. Skin and gore
All surgically clean and sparkling wet.
Whose? I have no idea. This isn't home.
On family beaches years ago I met
Old friends at crossroads traced in quartz and foam,
But those were different gems, another sea
Entirely. I have paddled or been blown
Or floated here. What's that? A shell? Off me?
An origin? A story? All that's known:
    I seem to be in pieces. We all are.
    Oh, everyone's a poet blah blah blah.

Ten.

Regarde Narcisse,
Regarde dans l'eau.
Regarde Narcisse,
Que tu es beau.

Oh, everyone's a poet blah blah blah.
I get it, we're all best in our own way.
Let's clear this up before it goes too far:
You sound like some millennial cliché.
Your art's degrading, that's what I can see.
Pandemic beauty breaks out. Boys and girls
Forgetting who to love and what to be.
This isn't worth my time. If these are pearls,
Then I'm a very irritated clam
Called Nemesis. I'm deadly. I may kill.
Stick that gem in your crown. *It's who I am.*
I can destroy you and perhaps I will.
    Don't cry. Your makeup's making you a clown.
    The snowflake trophy's ugly. Put it down.

Eleven.

The snowflake trophy's ugly. Put it down.
Come to the ocean's edge, the frozen shelf
Of waves that stand there while you try to drown.
Where water isn't, one can't see oneself.
The moment is a crystal. Clean as ice,
You see things in it. Future, present, past.
They're only images, and this device
As true or false as any. But at last
You're looking. Through a glass, a lens, a tool,
A telescope. At motion in the night
That's obvious enough to any fool
And blank to kings and men who must be right.
    Division bells replace us where we are.
    You're looking at the real thing: like, a star.

Twelve.

You're looking at the real thing: like, a star.
I'm old and made of absence. All burned out.
A fire once, raging. Hot. Now snuff and tar
In something's lungs. A putrid ball of gout
In something's feet. Because I was excess:
Too much, too soon. This constitution's frail
From eating like a queen and can't suppress
Its sickness any more. Fevered and pale
My planet's breaking up, waiting for death,
For time to stop. Its books are bodies too,
That bleed and burn and then run out of breath
And fall apart the same way women do.
    I float in space, a quiet ancient frown,
      Though I can't see much from inside this crown.

Thirteen.

Though I can't see much from inside this crown,
I do know adjectives. How more and less
Play well with what is finite. Any noun
Of higher order might evade their stress
But might explode. And might destroy our minds.
Talk binary to me? Even machines
Prefer it. Every anxious creature finds
Some peace in wins and losses, kings and queens,
Apples and oranges. I can compare
You to a summer's day or to a god,
Or daffodils or sealing wax. A pair
Of anythings will serve. Aren't couples odd?
    Well, even if they are they'll have to do.
    The point is: me first, then the rest of you.

Fourteen.

The point is: me first, then the rest of you.
Now *that's* a point. I'll say it once in Greek
And once in Latin so it's extra true.
It's time to speak of how one ought to speak.
In fact we should have started there. No, wait:
First, how to speak of how to speak of how.
Uh, how to speak of how to ... gosh it's late.
I think that covers everything for now.
The point is: this is madness and I'm mad.
The point is: going mad means you're on stage,
Your character has lines and can be sad
And breathe. And dance. And sing. And be the rage
    Of white men but refracted, second, new.
    This is the count of every thing. One, two.

Zero.

To win. To be the winner. Hey, it's me!
Toss me that apple and I'll sing a song:
"To be the chosen one or not to be."
Y'all who sang before me did it wrong.
What's happy if you're not the happiest?
A skin, a fig-leaf. Fashion for the Fall.
Let's ask Coco Chanel who wore it best.
Youth's beauty, beauty youth – and that is all.
Oh, everyone's a poet blah blah blah …
The snowflake trophy's ugly. Put it down.
You're looking at the real thing: like, a star,
Though I can't see much from inside this crown.
    The point is: me first, then the rest of you.
    This is the count of every thing. One, two.

Sappho Questions Medusa

0 (198B—C).

In which Sappho's poems are petrified before she has time to edit.
1 My words are rock, my lyrics turned to stone
2 just as I was about to trim them down.
3 I'm left to time, then, as too much of me.
4 (I'd run if there had been a where to run
5 to, out beyond the shrivelled space of now.)
6 A woman whose dark hair's a hissing crown
7 turned Gorgon eyes on me. (Has she seen you?)
8 (This is the count of every thing. One, two.)

1 (198D).

*And so we are left with a poet not in fragments but instead as
overabundance.*
1 My words got tangled in her snaky head
2 and I found myself giving up my dawn
3 my lyre my long transparent dress
4 my music and now there's too much of me
5 and of my words my songs myself my love ...
6 I tried to cut them back in life, in death,
7 because I knew well that I didn't know
8 the first thing about love. Poor, dear Sappho
9 who's too much left. But that's also, you see,
10 to be the winner. Paingiver. That's me.

2 (198E—199A).

What happens when a poet and a Gorgon have a love affair.

1 And as my lover turns my voice to stone,
2 the Gorgon bites into it like a peach
3 and chews and chews and chews
4   and
5   chews
6   and
7   chews
8 (What if your lover threw the pulp away
9 and ate only the seeds the peel the stem,
10 and what if that's the way she ate you, too,
11 would you feel like a tree that fruited wrong?)
12 Toss me that apple and I'll sing a song.

3 (199B).

And so as the Gorgon reads what her lover writes, and the eyes make love to the curves of the words, in those movements the poetry is petrified.

1 Rock worms crawl hard in the strata of me,
2 a rotting body that's rot's opposite.
3 I kiss my lover with a mouldy mouth
4 and try to breathe a poem in my kiss
5 while letters in my lungs go petrified
6 and each glass word rips tissue in its teeth,
7 a fossil of a phrasing of desire
8 as songs precipitate out from my flesh.
9 Break my body open when it's done
10 and read my love traced in the stony breath
11 and find the questions trapped there in my gut
12 and crack my stony bowel to pull them free
13 and hold them up like Yorick's skull to see:
14 And is this to be loved, or not to be?

4 (199C).

And the reader turns paleontologist digging for the bones of music in the stone, as the lover digging in the body of her beloved.

1 Gentle as you brush the crusted blood
2 from vowels knobbing from my bones, and gentle
3 while you split the muscle as it sheets
4 like mica from the rhyming in my thigh,
5 and gentle, please, be gentle as you bring
6 the cracking constant hammer down again
7 to try to loose the music from my teeth,
8 and gentle, as you pry them from my gums
9 and drop the jagged fragments in a jar
10 already white with love-bleached bits of flesh
11 that make a pretty tinkling when you shake.
12 What if a poem set like sediment
13 its lines its layers hardening with time
14 its verses hiding fossils in the sand.
15 What if we bury creatures in a song?
16 (Y'all who sang before me did it wrong.)

5 (199D).

So, dig. And ask your questions.

1 I watch the bits of sand drop into place
2 like jagged punctuation heaping piles
3 of stops and pauses stops and pauses stops
4 and stops and stops made out of little stones.
5 I follow their directions, one by one,
6 and stop. And stop. I stop. I stop. I pause,
7 I wait, I watch. A drop, a stop, I wait,
8 a drop, I watch. A geologic woman
9 marking time in sediment and breath
10 until the limestone like a mother heaves
11 her body metamorphic from the earth
12 as she gives marble birth to love deformed.
13 And whale bones stretch and pull her marble flesh,
14 her crystal belly chambers into vast

15 nautiloid hunger as it eats itself
16 alive, and watch I watch I rise I carve
17 new punctuation on this poet's breast.
18 What's happy if she's not the happiest?

6 (199E).

Now try to tell me about love.
1 What happens when you fossilize a voice?
2 Does it flake from the lungs in sheet
3 music played by the wind and birds and rain?
4 (She once dreamed of a dinosaur who tried
5 to sing a song to his beloved but
6 all he could make with his crocodile throat
7 were low deep booms and so his lover thrust
8 her listening head down deep into the sand
9 and it stayed there until some eager boy
10 from some eager time came with pick and knife
11 and chipped away her ears and put the bones
12 into his little eager bag and slung
13 the sound stones on his shoulder with his lunch
14 and drove away. And after she awoke
15 whenever she would open lips and throat
16 all that came out were low deep booms and so
17 she loved her lover like a crocodile
18 and breathed out reptile valentines, her skin
19 scaling to play the sounds her voice recalled.)
20 (Her skin's a purse, now. Fashion for the fall.)

7 (200A).

Then keep this object of love in mind, and remember what it is.
1 I see you, feathered serpent. Sweet winged snake,
2 who coils at me in seashells and in wind-
3 borne dust around my head that settles in
4 amid my braids and covers me in time.
5 Desire depends on absence of the one

6 desired, they tell me. So I sit alone
7 with neck craned up to spot my pterosaur,
8 remembering how I wove your hissing hair
9 into a writhing pair of wings, and how
10 I pressed into your head like clay and raised
11 a regal beaky crown. (Don't look at me,
12 my love: please turn around.) Quetzalcoatl
13 above me like a meteor demanding
14 sacrifice. What will you ask of me,
15 the woman waiting for you on the land,
16 if ever the sky lets you come back home.
17 Don't ask yourself what's likely, Socrates
18 said to a room once: think of what must be.
19 And so from sun to Socrates I turn,
20 and to necessity as my concern.
21 And when life wears me out, they'll find me dressed
22 in raggy wings I'll staple to my breast
23 when thinking of the love who wore them best.

8 (200B).

Presumably, no one is in need of those things he already has.
1 Before my body ages into stone
2 I'll open up my throat and sing for you
3 so that my voice creates a kind of time
4 that makes a kind of home where you can dwell.
5 And when the final beating of my heart
6 comes knocking on your door, you'll find me there,
7 a column like a tree gone petrified.
8 Come touch my bark and turn me on my side
9 and make a deep cut through the trunk of me
10 and close your eyes and run your fingers round
11 the sedimenting of my voice like tree
12 rings marking out the rich years and the lean
13 and play me like a record of what's been.
14 And will you, love, not then be satisfied?
15 Our story should have storms inside, you said.

16 Fulfilling a desire kills it dead.
17 Look upon the ocean when it roils
18 and metamorphosis is what you'll see.
19 Look upon the waters when they're still
20 and what you'll see is yourself staring back.
21 Though satisfaction calms the choppy seas,
22 let us be groping kraken in a squall
23 instead of honest mirrors on a wall
24 that smudge and crack and shatter when they fall.

9 (200C).

But maybe a solitary woman could want to be solitary.

We'll live inside a conch shell on a shore
and I can make my bed up at the tip
while you explore the water at the lip
and when my song twists toward you through the whorls,
the words accreting memories like pearls,
you'll string them up and wear them as a crown.

In cases like these, you might think people really do want to be things they
already are.

I'll find a crown-of-thorns starfish and string
the coral alveoli from my lungs
and drape the garland on the creature's spines
and crawl inside one of the little globes
so when you see the moonlight on the sea
you won't know that the tinsel's hiding me.

I bring them up so they won't deceive us.

You'll know of me the way you know of tinsel
coming into life in the earth's mantle
(amethysts and other fruits of trouble),
rising to the surface with the pebbles

doing just their darndest to be humble,
finding friends only amidst the fossils.

If you stop to think about them, you will see that these people are what they are,
whether they want to be or not.

I'll make my fossil friendships in the sand
while bits of me are crumbling into sand,
I'll give my spine to trilobites, the sand
will polish all my ribs and when the sand
is done the arthropods will swim through sand
to come and claim my bones.

And who, may I ask, would ever bother to desire what's necessary?

You'll live inside a cowry on the shore,
forgetting what your pearly crown was for.

10 (200D).
Whenever you say, **I desire what I already have,** *ask yourself*
whether you don't mean this:
1 To love, he said, is only to desire
2 the preservation of what one has now.
3 And so preserve me, lover. With your stare
4 you'll raise a fossil fauna from my ribs.
5 You look at me wiwaxic and the scales
6 grow skeletal upon me, spiny fingers
7 feather forth to brush across my bones.
8 Preserve me, keep me safe, glance at me
9 opabinic, sprouting stony stalky eyes
10 upon my feet to stretch and reach and look
11 upon you as you kill to keep me safe
12 from time from death from you. Preserve me, love.
13 Make me hallucinogenic from the needling
14 worms your vision makes from crack and crush
15 as they crawl from my mouth and craft a smile

16 of spike and prick fit only for your kiss.
17 And when I'm found in fragments years from now
18 they'll gather up what's left inside a box
19 and label it and put it on a shelf
20 until one afternoon an artist, bored
21 of this or that, will come to reconstruct
22 me in a spiny prehistoric story
23 of extinct morphologies of love.
24 With paint and ink she'll raise me from the dead
25 and bloom fantastic gardens from my flesh
26 and make of me a lost strange clan of beasts
27 that time herself refused to let go of.
28 And will you recognize me then, my love?

11 (200E).

For love is the love of something.

1 Desire, he said, wants what is not at hand.
2 So take my hand and cover it in gold
3 and set the flesh with crystal pressed from our
4 remembrances by heat and force of time
5 like diamonds crushed from carbon. Take my foot,
6 and plate the stone in silver, carve a hollow
7 to the bone, and crane your neck to peer
8 inside, rebuild my step in gilt and lead
9 and rubies. Clothe my morbid meat in glass,
10 love, make me monstrance, monstrous, make me more,
11 and love will have its object to adore.
12 Desire, he said, wants what is not in reach.
13 So reach for me and dance me out of death,
14 scoop all the dreams out from my hollow eyes
15 and skip them on the shadows like the stones
16 that once bounced on imaginary ponds
17 you conjured for us in your fantasies.
18 Then hold me, put your lips against my teeth
19 and with your tongue lap up the poetry
20 within my breathless throat, and drink it down

21 and sing the mourning winds into a storm,
22 and love will have its language and its form.
23 Desire, he said, wants what it can't possess.
24 So make a picture of me on the sand
25 and place my fragments each where they belong
26 and walk away as far as you can stand
27 and make a looking-glass out of your hand
28 and trace my constellation from afar
29 and let my bones help teach you who you are
30 and wish upon my absence like a star.

12 (201A).

The gods do not waste their love on ugly things.

1 The gods love what is beautiful, you said.
2 So fashion me like clay torn from the ground
3 and fire me like ceramic in a kiln
4 and glaze me like Palissy, take the snakes
5 still clutched within my fists, and take the serpents
6 writhing in my teeth from when we kissed,
7 and cover them in iron, tin, and lead,
8 and hold me in the flames until the crayfish
9 turn to angels, rainbows in my skin
10 reanimated by the heat within.
11 And if I burn out, it's all for the best:
12 I won't make so much trouble when you dress
13 me like a dish and hurl me to the sea
14 to sacrifice me to divinity.

13 (201B).

It turns out ... I didn't know what I was talking about in that speech.

1   you
2   fashion me
3 and fire me
4 and glaze me

5
6
7
8 and hold me
9   in my skin
10
11 And if I burn
12
13   hurl me to the sea
14 sacrifice me

14 (201C).

It is not hard at all to challenge Socrates.

1   you
2
3
4
5
6
7
8
9
10
11 burn
12
13
14   me

Quotation

I shall try to go through for you the speech about love I once heard from a woman. She is the one who taught me the art of love.

In some versions of the story, the girl does not know she will be sacrificed, believing instead that she is being led to the altar to be married.

You see, I had told her almost the same things Agathon told me just now. And she used the very same arguments against me that I used against Agathon.

In some versions of the story, she is transformed into an animal, or a priestess, or an immortal, and spared from death.

(No one asks her if she wants this.)

In some versions of the story, her father holds the little girl over the altar while her mother and her betrothed each beg for her life.

(Her mother does not succeed.)

(Her betrothed does not succeed.)

She showed me how, according to my very own speech, love is neither beautiful nor good.

In some versions of the story, later worshippers spare the virgins and instead whip a male victim, or draw blood from his throat, before an image of the goddess.

Watch your tongue, she told me.

In some versions of the story, the goddess strokes a deer, and watches, and waits.

Correct judgment, she said, has this character: it is in between understanding and ignorance.

Really, the story is not about the girl at all.

Don't force whatever is not beautiful to be ugly, or whatever is not good to be bad.

The story is about the brother, the father, the would-be groom.

Like the deer that replaces her, the girl is just a creature.

It's the same with love, she said. He could be something in between.

What is between girl and doe? Together they mark a beginning and an end, like quotation marks. What lies between (as between the sacrifice and the salvation, the father and the knife, the sister and the brother, the promise and the betrayal) is space for the voice of another.

Now do you see? she asked me.

"..."

(Look again. It's almost like the head of a doe, isn't it. It's almost like we're replacing the words with another creature to sacrifice, isn't it.)

What do you mean? I asked her.

And so where do the words go? Are they also spirited off to an island, thrust into the mouth of a priestess tasked with disposing of strangers who come seeking relief? And is that to save them? (And did it save the girl?)

It's a rather long story, she said. But she told it to me all the same.

And will someone also save Diotima at the last moment, as the philosopher brings the knife down on the stone?

How Xantippa caste pisse upon his heed.
This sely man sat stille as he were deed;
He wipte his heed, namoore dorste he seyn,
But 'Er that thonder stynte, comth a reyn!'
Geoffrey Chaucer

Blonde Horse

The unexamined woman, worth
my weight in faces. Shrew?
If I say so. I
bite. Put him in rags. *Stupid*
Nose. Stupid Face. Sting his arse,
limp shrimpy dick, stripped
white mess of belly, flap
it in my rich fingers. *Useless,*
poor. For this he pays me
his last cent. I sign
my receipts
X.

Myrto

One of your docile
animals. Said to have lacked
the necessities
of life.

To do list
Practise: strange
Practise: Maenad
Practise: fierce

Meanwhile
Socrates claimed to have two loves,
philosophy
and
Alcibiades.

Wow nice party Who's gonna clean up this mess
I'll tell you about Love Love is women's business
Clean it up Make me a sandwich Love me I deserve it OK but seriously Love is more
maintenance than you wanna know Like Love isn't a god she wears overalls and now
you think I mean Love's boring And that's the point man, that's the entire point
The work of keeping
Keeping house Keeping space Keeping time Women's work They're keeping it all
warm for you aren't they You know they're really not OK but listen I know a good
story Helenus learned prophecy from Cassandra he was her brother right But when
he predicted the future they believed him because
he just seems like he would know what he's talking about
So anyway Cassandra was crazy and her dark head growing all full of snakes and
the future It was not a gift it was a curse and it was because she wouldn't fuck Apollo
Crazy they said liar Liar LIAR and Lock her up and later they said Burn her and then
they said Rape her and Here's her address and her Social Security Number
I might have got this story in the wrong order, anyway Helenus was blond and good
and calm and not angry
just seems like he would know
So we talk about the Cassandra Complex We don't have a word for Helenus
Syndrome And another thing why is Love always endings Happy endings Tragic
endings Endings all the way down And here I am starting something
Sorry man
Didn't mean anything by it
Outta my orb

A Treasury of Incomplete Curses

The curses were recovered from the bottoms of wells, baths, and other watery places. Some were buried in craters in deserts that look alien in moonlight and one was inside a volcano. Most of the text has been lost on account of how language folded in on itself.

One.

Sweet   Nemesis listen
accept

precious gift
and I wore it once and my gems
first

and all my pretty hair bound
the boy with flowers

a rock

fingers
       mouth
my neck
and for

wrong may he

never open them again

unless a fire
skin like a diamond

unless

Two.

to reject such a beautiful
boy
ringlets

burned like nothing

air   his
speech
a fleece

but   I am
heavy
deflate and come down

mangled from the wreckage

Three.

out of his ears and his
yellow and foul-smelling
to make

and every woman
laughing at this

Four.

I have no coin for
                          these days
our gold stolen

If this man should
food it should choke
a horrid

with his bones sticking out

Five.

nothing nothing nothing nothing nothing

Six.

Goddess I beg you
go to him
sing
            pain in the extremities

slashing a harp string

Seven.

who ever took my

virgins
let
            hands that were never warm

shredding
preparing meals

in the bright nights when we scuttled

dark flowers and

the moon   her
now we   orbit
something else

Eight.

holly   a winter ago
we would crush
blood
licorice and ginger
in the night
you unfolded to me

        transforms

roots in a gold cup
flame   water

a cat with bright eyes, her voice

every tiny piece
and   chance

Nine.

I have come back
        violets
ivy and ribbons

cleverest and best-looking man

split right down the middle
and inside it's full

called me
the meanest flute girl
I think I would be happier if he were dead

can bite   tongue   shreds

courage
          take   care
in another fire of his own

Ten.

praying
with wings, my cries
like the fool in the proverb
I want

a new crown

piercing and crimson
speckles

share in   madness

unnaturally
rich   honey and spice
a soldier his   hands

drink and drink

death   hiding
its teeth

Static Transmission (2000 yrs, HD 1080p)

I painted this picture, painted the clouds as actual blood.
Edvard Munch

There was noise everywhere

What does noise look like
On the International Space Station there is a sunset every ninety
minutes
Most of them bloodless
How many dawns is too many
Do they become noise
Each orbit
a circular argument over who is moving,
who is staying still
Houston is still there
The Mississippi is still there
Same old Earth
Again
Again
Set
Rise

Ask a moon how it feels
about "down"

Time passes

everyone was made to start drinking

There is live video streaming
back at us from the Station

like a flashlight through an open door into a dark place
Is this light a friend
a terrible guardian
a teacher
a dead prayer
Is it to be trusted
[Who gets to make you start drinking]
Does it make the darkness down here darker

The primary purpose of this experiment we are told
[we may watch through a narrow window]
is not beauty
Is <u>not</u> beauty

the original guests

Ourselves perhaps
Look: our reflections in the narrow window
In the streaming light
In this glass of wine
[It is really not your party any more is it]
Losing form
Are we afraid
I have never been to Houston
I have never seen the Mississippi
These are our reference points

Aren't they

I don't say I know what we are
Can we breathe in space
Can we breathe in a tiny room
Are we afraid

their excuses
(it was winter, and the nights were quite long)
couldn't remember exactly what they were saying

We make meaning
from visual static
From snow
We make *we*
from visual static
Mostly grey

missed the first part
half-asleep anyway

But we will look for you
in these in-between spaces
(day and night
past and future
asleep and awake

authors should be able to write both comedy and tragedy

mythsleep and historysleep
truthmaidens and beautymaidens
sciencelanguage and artlanguage)

hardly able to follow his reasoning

Translating we recover (we discover)
the same old
Earth
only this sky is blood, this is wrong, otherly, alien
We might take another pass
A night falls every ninety minutes
Try again
Again
Again

Are we tired

drifted off

What problem do dreams solve

Dream sequence 1:
How Like a Goddess,
AKA The Beauty of the World

[but we are not your women]

washed up

Two thousand years later a shore finds you
(Diotima, Aphrodite, Nemesis, flute
girl)
It's an ice morning
You're going to need that shell to survive

Dream sequence 2:
Form and Moving
That was it
Or must we pick one

let's compromise

I feel like we already spoke with you about this
Is this our only chance, to feel
what a moon feels

we've seen through

We have read all the old books
Prisons for minds (theirs not ours)
Safe as houses
Same old Earth
spinning
A mindset every ninety minutes
How can a Station
move

How can static mean
we are here
Down here
Up here

in no particular order

There's only time's particular order
But it does
It makes do
It passes

What might be down there
come our next orbit
The next rediscovering

What might be up here

Afterword: Four Invitations to the Text

INVITATION: ON EXPERTS AND BEGINNERS

It's not typically the case that an invitation arrives after the event. But our invitations to you are also a means of reflection for us. These remarks are in that sense both backward-looking and forward-looking. A holding open of doors.

Both of us are trained in academic disciplines (philosophy, history) that emphasize the importance of argument, yet this is not a monograph with a thesis. Making meaning with a text does not necessarily look like proposing a thesis and arguing for it. One of the great joys of working with poetry and fiction is the ability to give material form to thoughts that are in the process of becoming, that are (always) beginnings, full of possibility, rather than endings, resolutions, closures. Poetry allows a writer to engage contradictory feelings without pressure to resolve or decide among them. Fictions have narrators and characters. Some of ours are denizens of dreams and nightmares. Some are not fully formed. They have indeterminate identities. Their relationships to each other and to characters of Plato's dialogue are unclear.

Both of us are trained to occupy an academic space by performing scholarly expertise, yet this is not a book that requires, expects, or desires a performance of such expertise on the part of either its readers or its writers. While we come to *Symposium* from different scholarly backgrounds, we come together, here, in the midst of similar re-orientations toward embracing our scholarly work as a serious-and-playful art practice.

Orienting toward scholarship as an art practice entails rethinking our relationship to expertise and asking questions of it. What, where, and how is expertise? What is it that we're trusting, when we trust an expert? And what is it that we're performing, when we perform expertise?

Claiming expertise is not a private act. Expertise is a form of social capital that builds relations by building boundaries. If we claim expertise, it is in relation to an object of attention (I am an expert in X), and to another who attends (I am an expert in X relative to others who are not). When we claim expertise, it is often *not* as a gesture of welcoming (come join me, let's talk) but instead as a hierarchical posture manifested in the construction of lines and gates and walls (I am in/up here and you are out/down there and you will listen to me).

Performing expertise is a choice. We aspire to be beginners.

In these poems, we choose not to write from positions of expertise or with the intention of claiming expertise for ourselves. Instead, we come to the text – and we offer the text to you, and we invite you also to come to the text – as beginners, as readers, as artists committed to engaging a work that interests and engages us by making something in conversation with it.

INVITATION: ON ORIGINS AND STORIES

One of this book's origin stories begins with the two of us teaching Plato's *Symposium* together to undergraduates at the University of British Columbia. Another begins slightly later, with us sharing wine and desperation by a fireside.

When you're teaching in the humanities, the question of what reading is, of what we're doing when we read something, becomes exceptionally important and exceptionally fraught. For some of us, writing is a way of reading. And writing with – or from – a text can be a way of reading it, of making it part of you, and of making yourself part of it. When we were teaching Plato's *Symposium*, we struggled. Where were we, in those pages? If there wasn't even room for a flute girl among the couches and the wine vessels, how could there be room for us?

For hundreds of years, to study philosophy was to be taught about men. Men's ideas, men's conversations, men's writing. Generations of professors found the absence of women's voices from the discipline no more remarkable than their absence from the *Symposium*.

In a classroom with other readers, as we were making our way together through the speeches of the philosophers on the couches, and as we came to those speeches in the course of a journey that had brought us there from earlier classroom encounters with Jocasta and Ophelia and Sappho, we found that many of the voices we heard in *Symposium* were voices that were silent in the text.

Silent voices in a text might be understood as undeveloped or unnoticed potential, as unacknowledged influences, as uninvited guests, or even ghosts. They might belong to the inhabitants of marginal spaces, relegated to action that takes place entirely offstage. If it's true that a text is a living organism, and if it's true that reading a text helps give it life (or lives, or afterlives), and if it's true that writing with a text is a way of reading it, then it seemed time to make new pages with new spaces where new voices in the *Symposium* could move. Our approach here is inspired by our desire to hear these silent voices and engage with them.

The present absence of Diotima in the *Symposium* is one way in. The most developed theory of love in *Symposium* is presented by Socrates, but he says he learned it from a woman. On the one hand, Diotima is here set on a rather extreme pedestal (who in the world would Plato depict as *wiser than Socrates*?) and on the other, she is permitted a place in the conversation only because she has inspired a man. (Intriguingly, this relationship sounds a gender-switched echo of the relationship between Apollo and the Delphic Oracle, the priestess who channelled his cryptic messages.)

But the topic where this happens is no accident: love has been considered *women's business* for thousands of years. When philosophy and academia gender themselves as male the very idea of a "philosophy of love" becomes its own kind of problem. A hot conceptual mess waiting to explode. Perhaps it's not a coincidence that there are volcanoes in our book. And stones and satellites and skulls.

Readers might wonder where all of that is coming from. We set ourselves the goal (we want to say the "task" but really it felt like a joy and a release) of voicing *Symposium* anew by writing in conversation with the original text, or at least with the translation thereof that we were teaching with. We each picked individual speeches to start with and took our own approaches to using the original speeches as a creative constraints. (When Plato's Socrates made a pun about a Gorgon's head at the end of Agathon's speech, for example, Medusa immediately came alive as a figure in the version of "Socrates Questions Agathon" included here, and she brought bodies full of stones with her.) In our text, then, we're playing with proximity: of our own writing to (a translation of) Plato, of the relationships of our pieces to each other, and ultimately of our work and play as writers, readers, and teachers. Alongside Plato, we were also discussing Anne Carson's *Autobiography of Red* with our students, and so volcanoes exploded into the work. And *Hamlet* brought skulls. And that's just the beginning.

We found ourselves writing through (or in, or because of, or about) a moment in time when movements like #MeToo and Time's Up brought sudden mass attention to an explosion of women's voices, making suddenly audible and unignorable how much molten pain and damage bubbles just below the hard, brittle surface of the world we're taught to call "normal." Academia is no different from Hollywood: too many academic "stars" have taken for granted their right to harass, creep on, and assault their women students and colleagues and are horrified by the idea of a future in which they will no longer be entitled to do this.

The individual poems all have their origin stories too. Although we each started out by working independently with separate sections of the original text (represented in the attribution of individual authorship to the poems), there were striking parallels and overlaps in our processes. So much was resonating between us when we were making these pieces. All of our pieces are making space (and spaces) with voice and voices and voicing.

Literary traditions reacting to systemic oppression often turn towards futurism, space travel, and other sci-fi tropes. In the closing sections of Plato's *Symposium* we found mentions of winter and night and sleepiness, as well as a strong sense of "zooming out." These things can translate themselves into images of the darkness, coldness, and vastness of space, and the "Final Dialogue" in our text is inspired partly by video images of Earth streamed live from the International Space Station. *Hamlet* snuck itself in there in the form of dream sequences, and the ways we had been playing with ideas of gender in earlier sections of the text began to materialize in the form of questions about the perspective of satellites and how a moon feels. In philosophy, women's work is easily eclipsed. We worked with a sense of cyclical motion, not only in space but also in time: feminism cycles through patterns of progress and pushback, much as the ISS looks down at the same world on each pass, although the clouds move around and the cities turn their lights on and off.

"The Speech of Phaedrus" was born in an attempt to use the process of writing to learn how to read the (translated) original. It began in a context of thinking and writing a lot about gods, and about the physical and conceptual metamorphoses that turn selves into gods and vice versa. One can find a creation story in Phaedrus's speech. But the story created a world that felt too cold, too focused on individuals, where women seemed merely instrumental. And so in "The Speech of Phaedrus" that world is undone, written as a decreation and an unmaking. Love's mother is transformed from an afterthought into a central voice. As you read her voice down the right side of the page, you'll hear her as she's framed by a translation of the dominant voicing of Plato's text down the left.

Plato's Aristophanes tells an origin story – a story that, itself, is widely considered to originate the idea of love as a coming together of "soulmates." As such, it has also become an origin for another story: the enduring myth that grounds "soulmate" love, even today, in a potent, damaging image of the single person as broken, incomplete, suffering. The "Before Aristophanes" poem emerged from a desire to reach back to before that picture got its claws into us, wanting to tell a more basic origin story about splitting and suffering. Many common methods for dealing with panic attacks employ forms of counting, and a simple count to ten became the structure of the story. The derealization that can accompany this kind of terror lends a warped sense of scale, and by passing through this warp effect it is possible to approach something as huge as Aristophanes's myth and talk back to it.

And if we stop here, it's only because stories always have to end.

The book was born in a classroom, and then it was born again in a living room (there was wine that time), and then it was born again in a Google doc, and then in readings and workshops. It's in this spirit of continual rebirth – of beginning, and beginning, and beginning – that we offer it to you. We are excited to think that it could spark other beginnings. Perhaps you have an interest in becoming part of the long history of making conversation with Plato's text. (We ourselves are interested in the idea of *talking back*. Is it disrespectful for a beginner to talk back to an expert?) Or maybe you are interested in paying attention to a text that's touched you, in a way that can only be processed by making art with it. (This was part of our motivation.) Or maybe your interests are completely otherwise. Whatever they might be, above all we welcome you to the text in this spirit of beginning and beginning and beginning. But (usually) something does not come from nothing, and beginnings can leave things broken in their wake. Being broken open is a way of becoming broken. Birth is bloody. If you've already read our poems you will have found blood on the pages.

We were both trained in academic disciplines that urged the leaving of one's feelings at the conference room door. There is not room in the article or seminar, we learned, for rage or grief, for overwhelming anxiety or ecstatic joy, for jumping or cursing. The lecturer is advised to put on her calm smiling skin before approaching the lectern. There are many ways of becoming broken.

Scholars are humans, and humans feel. Rage and joy and fear and passion and frustration are often what bring us to our objects of inquiry and draw the thoughts and words and voices from us. We work and think with our whole selves. We open ourselves to the world to pay the kinds of attention that help us to understand ourselves and each other more fully in the process. And attending to the world too closely, with eyes and skin and ears too open, is dangerous work.

Reading is one way of attending to the world, and like any practice of attention it is a creative act and it is a destructive act. It both breaks and makes. Our book is a reading of Plato. It is a translation, a commentary, a response, a reimagining, a celebration, a critique, and at the same time it is not properly any of these things. It is a bringing of our whole selves to a text to see what happens. Some of it is not pretty. Some of it is not intentional. We invite you to come to our text in the same spirit, if that interests you.

INVITATION: ON PLAY

The dictionary tells us that to play is to do something *rather than* something else. It is the opposite of something, ostensibly something serious or practical.

The origin of the word is apparently uncertain. It is "perhaps" this or that. Perhaps it is related to other words that mean to dance, to leap for joy, to rejoice, to be glad, to do things that children and young animals do. In this sense, to play means to do something with your body, to work, to exercise some part of your physical being, to be lively, capricious, to fly or spring, to gambol or flutter or flit, to frisk or fly or boil. To move freely in a space. To grant yourself the permission to spend your time doing that which might delight you.

Some creatures, like cats, never stop playing. Some people find this annoying.

In reading our book, we invite you to do the opposite of something, to spend time in the perhaps, in the actions your body might take before swarming. We invite you to read like a mayfly might read, or a grasshopper, or the fluffy bit of a dandelion that's just caught your breath.

We invite you to read like a cat. Or like The Fool – another beginner, always dancing on the precipice.

In our book, we invite you to play.